psalms & proverbs

v  y

Neighborhood Bible Studies Publishers
Dobbs Ferry, New York

Perspective and Wisdom for Today

Neighborhood Bible Studies
23 Discussions for Group Bible Study
Marilyn Kunz and Catherine Schell

Copyright ©1993, 1963 by Marilyn Kunz and Catherine Schell

ISBN 1-880266-05-9 (previous edition ISBN 0-8423-4991-X)
First Printing, June 1993
Printed in the United States of America
Cover by Tom Greene

CONTENTS

This study guide uses the inductive approach to Bible study. It will help you discover for yourself what the Bible says. It will not give you pre-packaged answers. People remember most what they discover for themselves and what they express in their own words. The study guide provides three kinds of questions:

1. What does the passage say?   What are the facts?

2. What is the meaning of these facts?

3. How does this passage apply to your life?

Observe the facts carefully before you interpret the meaning of your observations.   Then, apply the truths you have discovered to life today. Resist the temptation to skip the fact questions since we are not as observant as we think. Find the facts quickly so you can spend more time on their meaning and application.

The purpose of Bible study is not just to know more Bible truths, but to apply them. Allow these truths to make a difference in how you think and act, in your attitudes and relationships, in the quality and direction of your life.

Each discussion requires about one hour. Decide on the amount of time to add for socializing and prayer.

Share the leadership.   If a different person is the moderator or question-asker each week, interest grows and members feel the group belongs to everyone. The Bible is the authority in the group, not the question-asker.

When a group grows to more than ten, the quiet people become quieter. Plan to grow and multiply. You can meet as two groups in the same house or begin another group so that more people can participate and benefit.

Tools For An Effective Bible Study

1. A study guide for each person in the group.

2. A modern translation of the Bible such as:
    The New International Version (NIV)
    Good News Bible (GNB)
    Jerusalem Bible (JB)
    The New American Standard Bible (NASB)
    New English Bible (NEB)
    Revised Standard Version (RSV).

3. An English dictionary.

4. A map of the Lands of the Bible in a Bible or in the study guide.

5. Your conviction that the Bible is worth studying.

Guidelines For Effective Study

1. Stick to the passage under discussion.

2. Avoid tangents. If the subject is not addressed in the passage, put it on hold until after the study.

3. Let the Bible speak for itself. Do not quote other authorities or rewrite it to say what you want it to say.

4. Apply the passage personally and honestly.

5. Listen to one another to sharpen your insights.

6. Prepare by reading the Bible passage and thinking through the questions during the week.

7. Begin and end on time.

Helps For The Question-Asker

1. Prepare by reading the passage several times, using different translations, if possible. Ask God's help to understand it. Consider how the questions might be answered. Observe which questions can be answered quickly and which may require more time.

2. Begin on time.

3. Lead the group in opening prayer or ask someone ahead of time to do so. Don't take anyone by surprise.

4. Ask for a different volunteer to read each Bible section. Read the question. Wait for an answer. Rephrase the question if necessary. Skip questions already answered by the discussion. Resist the temptation to answer the question yourself.

5. Encourage everyone to participate. Ask the group, "What do the rest of you think?" "What else could be added?"

6. Receive all answers warmly. If needed, ask, "In which verse did you find that?" "How does that fit with verse...?"

7. If a tangent arises ask, "Do we find the answer to that here?" Or suggest, "Let's write that down and look for the information as we go along."

8. Discourage members who are too talkative by saying, "When I read the next question, let's hear from someone who hasn't spoken yet today."

9. Use the summary or application questions to bring the study to a conclusion on time.

10. Close the study with prayer.

11. Decide on one person to be the host and another person to be the question-asker for the next discussion.

The Psalms are the hymnbook and prayer book of Israel. These songs and prayers express a vividly personal relationship with God, and range in emotion from great joy to deep sorrow, from penitence and confession of sin to rejoicing and praise to God. The Psalms reveal the character of people and the nature of God.

Sometimes the *I* is the spokesperson for the worshiping people. Many psalms originated in a personal setting and were later gathered together for public use in the sanctuary and in homes. Others were originally composed for use in group worship.

Hebrew poetry achieves rhythm largely by repetition of ideas, called parallelism. Three kinds of parallelism are:

1. Synonymous. The second half of a verse repeats the identical thought of the first part in different words. *The LORD is my light and my salvation— whom shall I fear? The LORD is the stronghold of my life—of whom shall I be afraid?* (Psalm 27:1).

2. Antithetic. A contrast is stated in the second clause. *For the LORD watches over the way of the righteous, but the way of the wicked will perish* (Psalm 1:6).

3.   Synthetic. The thought is developed or enriched by the second clause (a) as a consequence: ***The LORD is my shepherd, I shall not be in want*** (Psalm 23:1), or (b) as an expansion: ***Surely goodness and love will follow me all the days of my life, and I will dwell in the house of the LORD forever*** (Psalm 23:6).

This rhythm of sense affects the way we interpret a psalm. Within a verse the thought of the first line is continued, enlarged, or modified by the following line(s). Therefore, to find the meaning we must take the verse and not the single line as the unit of expression.

Christians from the first century onward have used the Psalms in their personal and public worship.

A Definition of the Happy Person

Psalm 1

Many people think of life as a pursuit of happiness. Modern advertising conditions us to think in terms of pleasure, satisfaction, 'and happiness. In this psalm we have God's definition of the blessed or happy person, set over against a description of the opposite way of life. Every person is described, either in the first or second half of this psalm.

Read Psalm 1:1-3

1. What negative and positive statements describe the happy person?

   What deepening of association do the verbs in verse 1 indicate?

   How is this progression true in life?

2. What is the significance of the series—wicked, sinners, scoffers?

   What do people scoff or scorn today?

3. What does the blessed person do?

Note: **The law** *(torah)* **of the LORD** *is really <u>the instruction of the LORD</u>. For a glimpse of its importance to the godly Jew, read Joshua 1:7, 8; and Jeremiah 31:33.*

4. What two responses does the happy person have toward God's law?

5. In the rapid pace of modern life, few learn the art of meditation. Look up *meditate* in the dictionary. What are some practical ways to develop the ability to meditate?

6. As a result of delighting in and meditating on the law, what is the happy person like (verse 3)?

    What qualities of life and character does this picture imply?

Read Psalm 1:4-6

7. What contrast is made between the godly person and the wicked (verses 3, 4)?

    What is **chaff**?

    What qualities of life and character are implied by this description?

8. Jeremiah 17:5-8 also contrasts the wicked and the godly. What additional insights does it give you about each type of person?

9. What future do the wicked have?

10. What is the difference between the two ways of life?

Summary

1. What does this psalm show about the importance of the company you keep? Illustrate from today's world.

2. From the contents of current magazines, what things delight your generation?

   What difference would it make if a person delighted in the law of the LORD (verse 2)?

3. What prescription would you suggest for someone in search of true happiness?

Psalms & Proverbs

Two Witnesses to God

Psalm 19

When you want to get to know someone or when you are trying to describe one person to another, you concentrate on what the person does and what he or she says. Actions and words reveal a person's character and ability. This psalm deals with God's expression of himself, introducing himself by his work (the material universe) and by his word (the law).

Read Psalm 19:1-6

1. What words describe the function of the heavens (verses 1-4)?

    What times and places are mentioned in connection with this activity?

2. How do the heavens speak without speech or words or voice?

    What do they say?

3. What pictures do the similes about the sun suggest (verses 4c-6)?

4. Why must all people know something about God (verses 4, 6)?

5. What do the heavens reveal to you about God?

Read Psalm 19:7-14

6. The psalmist now turns his attention from nature to God's law. How does he describe the law or commands of God (verses 7-9)?

   What impresses you about the description?

7. What four things does the law do for a person (verses 7,8)?

   In each case, what need is met?

8. What two things does the psalmist contrast with the LORD's will (verse 10)?

   How and why are the law and ordinances of the LORD superior to the things we expect to bring us happiness?

9. What experiences have convinced you that God's will and laws are for your highest good?

10. What two effects do the law and ordinances of the LORD have upon the writer in verse 11?

    What relationship does he have with the LORD?

11. To what realization does the psalmist come in verse 12?

As a result, what four petitions does he make in prayer (verses 12-14)?

12. How would you define **hidden faults** and **presumptuous (RSV)** or **willful sins**?

    Why may they sometimes rule over a person?

Note: George Macdonald said, "Man's first business is, 'What does God want me to do?' not 'What will God do if I do so and so?'"

13. How may a person be **blameless, innocent,** and **pleasing** in God's sight?

    What does it reveal about the LORD that he is called **my Rock and my Redeemer**?

Summary

1. This psalm moves from the vastness of the heavens to the inner thoughts of a person's heart. What does it reveal about what God does and what he says?

2. If you knew only this psalm, what would you know about the relationship between God and human beings?

3. Verse 14 is a good verse to memorize. Write it on a card and place it above your kitchen sink, office desk, mirror, or other obvious place for a week. Read it, think about it, memorize it and pray it.

Psalms & Proverbs

Security

Psalm 23

Today, the world lives in a continual state of insecurity about its very existence. The environment is endangered by industrial pollution and overpopulation. Political unrest explodes into guerrilla and border wars in Europe, the Middle East and Far East.

To such a time, this psalm, the most dearly loved chapter in the Old Testament, speaks with amazing relevance. To know true security we must know the LORD, the shepherd of the psalmist. Before reading this psalm make a list of all the things which a sheep needs. Remember that in the animal kingdom sheep are noted for their defenselessness, stupidity, and instability.

Read Psalm 23:1-4

1. What basic relationship does the psalmist have with the LORD?

2. Why is David not in want?

What four specific things does the LORD do for him?

Translate these provisions into terms of human need.

3. Note a change from *he* to *you* in verse 4. To whom does David now speak directly?

    What do you think this indicates?

4. In what extreme condition does David know security? Why?

5. The rod was an instrument of discipline, the staff an instrument of guidance and rescue for the sheep. In what ways do the LORD's rod and staff provide comfort for you as well as for David?

Read Psalm 23:5,6

6. In this section, what picture is drawn?

    What relationship is revealed between the psalmist and the LORD?

7. What aspects of life are suggested by the things which the LORD as host provides so bountifully?

8. What assurance does David have for the future?

    Why, do you think, is he able to speak with such confidence?

Summary

1. In what ways have you ever felt like the LORD's sheep or his guest?

2. In verse 1 the psalmist speaks of no **want** or *lack*; in verse 4 he speaks of no *fear of evil*. To live without fear or want would certainly be security. In each case, however, upon what does this security depend? Why?

3. In the light of Psalm 23, read aloud John 10:7-15. How is this an answer to your own need for security?

A Psalm for Times of Fear

Psalm 27

F ear, a most destructive emotion, paralyzes and destroys. Apprehension, anxiety and worry describe facets of fear in the human mind and heart. The Bible speaks against all fear except the reverent awe for God. He alone is worthy of our fear. In this psalm you'll see how a person deals with fear honestly and courageously.

Read Psalm 27:1-3

1. What three pictures of God does the psalmist use in verse 1?

    Why is he not afraid?

2. In verses 2 and 3, what three situations does the writer describe?

    What is the result in each case?

3. Do you think he is boasting when he says, *When ..., though ..., even then will I be confident*?

Read Psalm 27:4-6

4. In these verses what specifically will the psalmist do?

    What will the LORD do?

5. How does each depiction of the dwelling place or presence of God in verses 4-6 describe a different facet of David's experience?

6. In this time of trouble and danger what is David's chief desire in life?

    How would such a viewpoint help you to deal with fear in your life?

Read Psalm 27:7-12

7. What changes do you notice in these verses compared with the first six verses of the psalm?

    What encourages David to pray?

8. What are his petitions (verses 7-12)?

    What do they reveal about his fear?

9. Verse 10 expresses the desperate need of an abandoned child. What is David's cry under these circumstances?

10. How does David acknowledge his need for guidance?

    Why is much of your anxiety based on not knowing which way to go?

Read Psalm 27:13, 14

11. Put David's statement of faith (verse 13) into your own words.

    What advice does the psalmist give himself and others?

12. What part do faith, waiting, and courage play in combating fear?

13. For whom is the psalmist waiting?

    What difference does this make?

Summary

1. What are the most common fears people have today?

   How do you handle these fears?

2. Read the entire psalm, consciously putting yourself into the place of "I" throughout. Each person can read silently, or one can read aloud while all listen.

Overwhelmed by an Awareness of Sin

Psalm 38

When Jonathan Edwards read the Scripture and preached in New England in the eighteenth century, men and women by the score fell prostrate, overwhelmed by the awareness of their sin and guilt before God. Conviction of sin still grips those who recognize the holiness and righteousness of God and their own guilt before him. This psalm exposes what sin can do to a person. Notice that the writer deals with the awareness of sin by prayer, not by denying or minimizing his guilt.

Read Psalm 38:1-8

1. To whom is David speaking and what is his plea?

   How does he describe his great physical and moral distress? Notice the repetition of *I* and *my*.

2. The psalmist not only describes his condition but he states certain reasons for it. What are these reasons (verses 3, 4, 5, 8)?

3. If the writer were your contemporary, how would you describe his condition to a friend?

Read Psalm 38:9-14

4. It may be that this psalm was written when David's sin with Bathsheba (see 2 Samuel 11, 12) became known. How does humiliation add to the burden of one's sin?

5. What affects has all this had on David's friends?

    How has it affected his enemies?

    How has it affected David himself?

6. What element of hope do you see in this section?

7. To what longings and sighings do you think David refers in verse 9?

    Even in the depths, being overwhelmed by the awareness of one's sin and dumbstruck with shame because others know about it, what is left?

Read Psalm 38:15-22

8. How has the focus of David's attention shifted?

9. What new attitude does the psalmist now exhibit toward his sin?

    What do you learn about his enemies' behavior (verses 16, 19, 20)?

10. What change has come over David as he prays (verses 21, 22 and 1, 2)?

    To understand these four verses better, think of them in terms of your own children's pleas to you.

Which of the two requests would you rather hear? Why?

11. How does the final phrase of this psalm answer the problem of sin and guilt for a person?

What answer does 1 John 1:5-10 give?

Summary

1. In verses 1, 9, 15, 21, 22, David addresses God. What progress in faith do you see in these prayers?

2. In the light of the psalm, what does it mean to call the LORD *my Savior*, or *my salvation (RSV)* (verse 22)?

Psalms & Proverbs

The Emotions of Liberation

Psalm 40

The joy of deliverance is a rare commodity. This psalm describes the experience of the soul delivered from spiritual bondage by the mercy and grace of God.

Read Psalm 40:1-5

1. What one thing did the psalmist do?

    What six things did the LORD do for him (verses 1-3)?

    How do you visualize the rescue pictured here?

2. What is involved in waiting patiently for the LORD?

3. How desperate was the situation from which God rescued him?

    How complete was his restoration?

4. What connection do you see between trust (verses 3b, 4) and waiting (verse 1)?

How long are you willing to wait patiently?

5. How does the psalmist sum up his experience in verse 5 ?

Read Psalm 40:6-10

6. What conclusions does the psalmist reach about the worship of the LORD?

   Why is ritual not the essence of true worship?

7. In what five ways does the writer describe his actions as a liberated soul (verses 9, 10)?

   How are these testimonies of thanksgiving also worship?

8. What four qualities of God's deliverance does the Psalmist recognize (verse 10)?

   Which of these qualities have you recognized in God's working in your life?

Read Psalm 40:11-17

9. Having made three statements of what he has not done (verses 9, 10), what plea does the writer now make in verse 11?

10. What problems face the psalmist from within?

    What problems face him from without?

    After such a deliverance as that in verses 1-3 and his consequent praise to God, the godly person often experiences special persecution and renewed awareness of sin. How does the psalmist handle these new troubles?

11. What personal requests or petitions does the writer make (verses 11-15)?

   What are his enemies plotting?

12. Upon whom does the psalmist pray blessings (verse 16)?

13. What thought overwhelms the psalmist in verse 17?

14. Compare the final plea in verse 17 with the opening phrase of the psalm. Why must there always be new experiences of waiting and trust for the child of God?

Summary

1. What do you learn about the Lord as you see him through the psalmist's eyes?

2. This Psalm describes the cycle of *joy* over deliverance followed by *dedication* to God and *witness* about him to others, then a *new awareness* of personal *sin* and *problems* from without, a new *cry* for help and a new time of *waiting* patiently.

   How does God use all these things to bring you closer to him?

Perspective in Bad Times

Psalm 46

Facing threats on his life, Martin Luther, inspired by this psalm, wrote the majestic hymn "A Mighty Fortress Is Our God." To many, small and great, this psalm has brought strength throughout the ages. In any circumstance, it makes a difference to know the one in charge.

Read Psalm 46:1-3

1. What is the meaning of the great declaration with which this psalm begins?

    What separate thoughts does each word convey?

2. What is the one result of verse 1?

    What does fear do to a person?

    Think of recent situations in which refuge, strength, and help were sorely needed.

3. What four terrifying possibilities does the psalmist consider?

4. The description here of chaos in nature may also refer metaphorically to political international upheaval. Why, in the midst of chaos and calamity, does this section still create an atmosphere of stability?

    How can a person enjoy this same stability?

Read Psalm 46:4-7

5. Discover all the contrasts you can between verses 2, 3 and 4, 5.

    If you were painting these verses in two different pictures what colors and style would you use in each?

    How would the sea (verses 2, 3) be different from the river (verse 4)?

6. Who is mentioned in nearly each phrase of this section?

    In each case what action or situation is described?

7. If verses 2, 3, 4, 5 were the description of a person, what difference does God's presence make to the personality?

8. What contrast does verse 6 suggest between the activities and power of people and that of God?

*Note: **the earth melts** refers to an earthquake.*

Read Psalm 46:8-11

9. What are the commands in this section?

Why this sequence?

10. To what aspect of God's work does the writer direct our thoughts?

    Why is the realization of God's power and authority in these realms a source of comfort and strength in days of international turmoil?

11. Why does the psalmist not stop with the contemplation of God's works?

    What contrast would you make between verses 9 and 10 if you were making a sound track of these verses?

12. Why must we experience inner stillness to be able to know God's presence in trouble?

13. What is the meaning of *refuge* and *fortress* (verses 1, 7, 11)?

    The LORD of hosts *(RSV)* or **The LORD Almighty** speaks of God's divine power as ruler of the heavenly armies or of stars and planets. **The God of Jacob** is a reminder of God's covenant of love.

    How are these two things just what you need in times of trouble?

Summary

1. How have God's sovereignty and love affected your life in times of deep distress?

2. Read aloud Martin Luther's hymn, "A Mighty Fortress Is Our God."

Note: *"Lord Sabaoth" is an older translation of* **LORD of hosts.**

A mighty Fortress is our God,
A Bulwark never failing;
Our Helper He amid the flood
Of mortal ills prevailing:
For still our ancient Foe
Doth seek to work us woe;
His craft and power are great,
And, armed with cruel hate,
On earth is not his equal.

Did we in our own strength confide,
Our striving would be losing;
Were not the right Man on our side,
The Man of God's own choosing:
Dost ask who that may be?
Christ Jesus, it is He;
Lord Sabaoth His Name,
From age to age the same,
And He must win the battle.

And though this world, with devils filled,
Should threaten to undo us;
We will not fear, for God hath willed
His truth to triumph through us:
The Prince of Darkness grim,
We tremble not for him;
His rage we can endure,
For lo! His doom is sure,
One little word shall fell him.

That word above all earthly powers,
No thanks to them, abideth;
The Spirit and the gifts are ours
Through Him who with us sideth:
Let goods and kindred go,
This mortal life also;
The body they may kill;
God's truth abideth still,
His Kingdom is forever.

Psalms & Proverbs

Need for Restoration

Psalm 51

If you don't know how or what to pray, if you don't feel like praying, if you have no sense of fellowship with God, pray this psalm through with your whole heart. You will experience restoration. God will respond according to his steadfast love and abundant mercy.

Read Psalm 51:1-12

1. What is the occasion for the psalm as described in its title?

   For background see 2 Samuel 12:1-14.

2. What is David's need?

   Upon what does David base his requests?

3. What does he understand about the nature of his sin?

   What does he understand about his own sinful nature?

4. What attributes of God does he mention in verses 1-4?

    How are these relevant to David's situation?

5. What does David understand about himself and God (verses 5, 6)?

6. On the basis of this understanding, for what does he plead beyond forgiveness (verses 7-9)?

    In each instance who is the active one and who is the passive one?

*Note: Under Mosaic law, **hyssop** was the plant whose twigs were used to sprinkle blood upon the person being cleansed from sin or defilement. There was also a cleansing with water.*

7. From his concern with cleansing from sin, to what does David's attention move (verses 8, 10-12)?

    What relationship is he afraid of losing? Why?

Read Psalm 51:13-19

8. What does David pledge to do because of his restoration?

9. What kinds of sacrifice please God and are acceptable to him?

10. Why is such sacrifice both the forerunner and the natural outcome of restoration in our relationship with the Lord?

How can you offer sacrifices to God that are acceptable to him?

Note: For sacrifices of righteousness, see Hebrews 13:15, 16.

11. Verses 18, 19 were probably added later to David's psalm to adapt it for public worship, possibly after the exile in Babylon when Jerusalem's walls were broken down and sacrifices had ceased. How does the Psalm seem an appropriate expression of the confession of a disobedient nation?

Summary

1. David was a man who knew what it was to have fellowship with God. How and why was his fellowship broken?

   How and why was it restored?

2. David acknowledged that everything he did, even his sin, involved him with God. From this prayer psalm, what do you learn about God with whom David wanted restored fellowship?

   What does 1 John 1:5-10 add to your understanding of restored fellowship with God?

When Evil People Seem To Prosper

Psalm 73

"How do they get away with it?" Perhaps it is a notorious gangster or a power-hungry labor leader, a dishonest landlord or a malicious social climber. Seeing such people succeed troubles us. Where is God's justice? Where is God? The writer of this psalm faced this same problem centuries ago.

Read Psalm 73:1-9

1. What does the psalmist believe about God?

    Because he believes this, what problem does he face?

    What is this godly man tempted to do?

2. From what are the wicked apparently exempt (verses 4-9)?

    What are they like?

Read Psalm 73:10-20

3. What doubts and questions have begun to haunt those who observe the success of the wicked?

4. What effects has the prosperity of the wicked had upon the psalmist?

   What complaint does he make?

5. Follow the readjustment of the psalmist's thinking in verses 15-17 by tracing the words *If, When, till, then*. Where does the turning point occur?

   When and to whom is it wise to voice our struggles?

6. What new understanding does the psalmist reach (verses 18-20)?

   How is it different from what he thought he saw in verses 6-9?

Read Psalm 73:21-28

7. As the psalmist looks within and searches his own heart, what does he realize (verses 21-26)?

   Why was his previous attitude so dangerous (verses 21, 22)?

   Why does every bitterness in our hearts always alienate us from the Lord?

8. Of what four things is the psalmist confident (verses 23, 24)?

9. What choice does the psalmist make in verses 25, 26?

   What would this stand of faith do to his attitude of verse 3?

10. In verses 27, 28, what contrasts are drawn between the ungodly and the godly?

    Why is our relationship to God the truly important factor in life?

Summary

1. Why do we sometimes lose proper perspective when we observe injustice?

    How can we regain a right perspective?

2. How can you use this psalm in counseling your children when they see or face injustice?

For further study on this subject, see Psalm 37.

The Prayer of the Poor and Needy

Psalm 86

Prayer includes the many ways we communicate with God including: worship (honoring God for who he is), praise (acknowledging all that God has done), confession, petition, intercession (petition in behalf of others), and thanksgiving. You will find most of these elements in this prayer psalm, which expresses the heart's desperate cry for help from the Lord.

Read Psalm 86:1-7

1. What are the psalmist's eight petitions in verses 1-7?

    How would you summarize his plea in your own words?

2. Why does the psalmist think his requests should be granted?

3. What relationship exists between the writer and God?

    What does he understand about God's character?

Read Psalm 86:8-13

4. What reasons does the writer give for his worship and praise to God in verses 8-10?

    Why are the words *none* (verse 8), *all* (verse 9), and *alone* (verse 10) so important?

    Why is it essential that we remember such things about the One to whom we pray?

5. What similarities do you notice between verse 9 and Philippians 2:9-11?

6. Why does the Psalmist make the two requests in verse 11?

    What difference would it make in one's life to have an undivided heart?

7. How and why are thanks expressed in verses 12 and 13?

Read Psalm 86:14-17

8. What immediate problem faces the writer?

    How are his enemies described?

    What implies that they are God's enemies as well?

9. How do the psalmist's enemies differ from the LORD (verses 14, 15)?

10. In view of his current situation what requests does the psalmist make?

Note: **son of your maidservant** *implies the relationship of a slave born in the household claiming protection from his master.*

11. What will happen to the psalmist's enemies? Why?

    How will this help to fulfill verses 9 and 12?

Summary

1. Although the requests in this prayer relate to personal need, notice that they are based only upon the character of God, his truth, his name, his love, his forgiveness, and upon this man's relationship to him. Why can God answer such a prayer as this?

2. Close your study with sentence prayers of worship and praise by reading verses 5, 8-10, 12, 13, and 15.

The Time of Your Life

Psalm 90

Moses wrote this psalm, the oldest in the Psalter, probably during Israel's wandering in the wilderness where those who had stubbornly refused to believe and obey God were sentenced by him to die without entering the promised land. The psalm's broader application reminds us of the gap between the eternal and the temporal. People are always concerned with time, especially their own length of life, but Moses emphasizes the quality and significance of life rather than its length.

Read Psalm 90:1-6

1. What references to time do you find throughout this psalm?

2. What two facts are revealed about God from the first two verses of the prayer?

   What does each of these facts emphasize?

3. How is man contrasted with God in verses 3-6?

Read Psalm 90:7-12

4.   How does the mood in verses 7-10 differ from the mood in verse 1?

What apparently accounts for this change of mood (verse 8)?

5.   What impresses you about this description of life?

6.   What troubles the writer (verse 11)?

What is the proper response to God's anger?

7.   What request does meditation upon these things cause the psalmist to make?

What does it mean to **number our days**?

What practical difference would it make in your life to do this?

8.   Why may a mere **numbering of our days** without **gaining a heart of wisdom** bring tragedy?

What further insights do you get from Ephesians 5:1, 2, 15-17?

Read Psalm 90:13-17

9.   How does the tone of the prayer change again in this section?

What specific requests does the psalmist make on behalf of God's servants?

10. What would you know about God from verses 13-17 if you had no other part of the Bible?

11. What does the psalmist consider an evidence of God's favor (verse 17)?

    How does this prayer for permanence *(establish)* compare with the prevailing atmosphere of the psalm?

12. What kind of *work* (verse 17) could you ask the LORD to establish? Why?

    What does Colossians 3:17, 23-25 teach about the significance of work?

Summary

1. How may this Psalm's perspective on the length of life benefit you?

2. What helps you remember that eternity is as real as time?

A Song of Confidence

Psalm 91

This psalm declares great promises from God and the conditions for claiming them. Traditionally, the psalm has comforted soldiers in war, but you will also find help here in the ordinary battles of life. You might send it as a letter of encouragement to a hurting friend.

Read Psalm 91:1-8

1. To whom are the promises of verses 3-8 addressed?

    What does it mean to *dwell* and to *rest* (verse 1)?

2. What three things will the LORD be to the one who fulfills the conditions of verse 1?

    What confidence does this person have?

3. What attributes of God are described in verses 3,4?

    Why is there need of his protection (verse 3)?

4. Why does the experience of verses 5, 6 follow the faith expressed in verse 2?

What happens when fear possesses an individual?

5. What indicates that the dangers are very real and not just imaginary problems (verses 7, 8)?

    What division between people is suggested here?

Read Psalm 91:9-13

6. How can God be your *refuge* or *dwelling*?

    How does verse 9 build upon the thoughts of verse 1?

7. What new promises are made (verses 10-13) based upon verse 9?

    What new areas or conditions are described?

Read Psalm 91:14-16

8. Who apparently is the speaker in this last portion of the psalm?

    What effect does this divine interruption have upon the mood of the psalm?

9. What condition is placed upon the promises?

    What do the conditions mentioned in verse 14 add to those stated in verses 1 and 9?

10. What are the promises in verses 14-16?

    What areas of human need do they cover?

How are these areas of need addressed in Romans 8:28, 38, 39?

Summary

1. What picture do you get of the person described in verses 1, 2, 9, 14?

2. What things must you do if you want to receive the benefits promised in this psalm?

3. Where do people look for refuge today?

   In the final analysis, where can a person find safe refuge?

A Psalm of God's Love and Mercy

Psalm 103

Psychiatry strongly affirms our need to be loved. It emphasizes the terrible plight of the person who is not loved, or who does not know that he or she is loved. Many people think in terms of being worthy of love, spending vast amounts of energy trying to earn love. But this psalm declares that God's love and mercy are based on his character, not on our worth. Our security rests on the eternal character of God.

Read Psalm 103:1-5

1. As the psalmist addresses himself, what two things does he tell himself to do?

2. What five things reveal the love and mercy of God to the psalmist?

    How would you describe the conditions from which he is rescued?

3. From these verses what do you know of this man?

    With which of these experiences can you personally identify?

Read Psalm 103:6-10

4. As the psalmist considers all that God has done for him personally, he begins to review God's gracious dealings with his people, the nation of Israel. How has God dealt with Israel (verses 6-10)?

    What additional insights do you gain from Joshua 24:5-8, 11-13?

5. If you had only these five verses out of the whole Bible, what would you know about people?

    What would you know about God?

    What would you know about the relationship between God and human beings?

Read Psalm 103:11-18

6. What does each of the three similes or pictures of God's love and mercy reveal (verses 11-13)?

7. In verses 14-18 what contrasts does the writer draw between God and human beings?

8. What are the conditions for receiving God's love and mercy (verses 11, 13, 17, 18)?

9. *Fear* here means a reverence of God's authority, causing a person to obey God's commandments. To *keep his covenant* means to obey his commandments. What motivation for fearing and obeying God do you find in Deuteronomy 7:6-11?

    How can you evaluate the extent to which you fear God and keep his covenant?

Read Psalm 103:19-22

10. What new thought does the psalmist add here about God?

    Whom does he call to join in praise?

11. In this section how does the psalmist show the necessity of personal as well as universal praise for God's love and mercy?

Summary

1. What does this psalm teach about the character of God?

    How does the quality of his love differ from other loves?

2. Considering verse 2, make a list of all God's benefits to you. Selections from each person's list can be read as a closing prayer of thanksgiving.

    You may want to use your list as a reminder for specific thanks and praise to God in your personal daily prayers this week.

A Human Being in Relation to God's Will

Psalm 119:1-16

Distinguished as the longest chapter in the Bible, this Psalm is also an outstanding example of an acrostic poem. Each letter of the Hebrew alphabet (twenty-two in all) begins eight successive verses. This is the most complete statement in the Bible on the importance and relevance of the expressed will or law of God. This study examines the first two sections of the psalm.

Read Psalm 119:1-8

1. What conditions for happiness or blessedness are given in verses 1-3?

2. Why would walking in the law and ways of the LORD and keeping his testimonies make one happy?

   What does this indicate about human beings?

3. To whom are verses 4-8 addressed?

   What requests and what vows does the psalmist make?

Why are the vows encased in prayers for help?

4. When does the psalmist move from general to personal statements?

    Why is this transition always necessary for a person dealing with God's will?

Read Psalm 119:9-16

5. What issue or problem is raised in verse 9?

    What is the answer to it?

6. Kierkegaard, the famous Danish philosopher of the nineteenth century, said, "Purity of heart is to will one thing." How does this statement compare with the psalmist's words in verses 9, 10?

7. In verses 11-16 what does the psalmist say he has done?

    What he is doing?

    What he will do?

8. What two prayers for help does the psalmist make?

    What does each indicate about the writer?

9. How and why would a person hide God's word in his or her heart?

10. What do the words *praise* (verse 7), *rejoice* (verse 14) and *delight* (verses 16) indicate about God's will?

Summary

1. List all the words in verses 1-16 which are used as synonyms for God's will.

    What idea does this list give you of the kind of person God is?

2. What practices or attitudes from this psalm promote happiness?

God and You

Psalm 139

The English poet Francis Thompson wrote "The Hound of Heaven" based on this psalm, particularly verses 7-12. The poem tells the story of a person who tries to find satisfaction outside of God. Each of these avenues fails but the Hound of Heaven never ceases to pursue. In the final portion the Lord speaks:

"Lo, all things fly thee
For thou fliest Me!
Strange, piteous, futile thing!...

Alack, thou knowest not how little worthy of any
    love thou art!
Whom wilt thou find to love ignoble thee, save Me,
    save only Me?
All which I took from thee I did but take, not for
    thy harms,
But just that thou might'st seek it in my arms, all
    which thy child's mistake fancies as lost,
I have stored for thee at home : Rise, clasp My
    hand, and come."

Read Psalm 139:1-6

1. What specific things does God know about *me*?

    What areas of life are covered by God's knowledge?

2. What else does God do besides know me?

    What does this tell you about God?

3. How does the psalmist react to the realization of these things?

    What attributes of God have been implied in this section?

4. What does it mean to you to realize that the LORD God knows all about you, and that he acts in your life?

Read Psalm 139:7-12

5. How does the writer react to the awareness of God's intimate knowledge of him?

6. Why would every way of escape from God fail?

*Note: In verse 8 <u>hell</u> or **Sheol** is the grave, or the abode of the dead.*

7. What relationship is pictured in verse 10?

    In what ways do people today actually try to escape from the knowledge and presence of God?

    How successful are these attempts?

Read Psalm 139:13-18

8. What new things does the psalmist realize in this section?

9. The psalmist wants to flee when he realizes God's full knowledge of him (verses 1-6) and God's constant presence with him (verses 7-12). How is this desire relieved by what he comes to understand in verses 13-18?

*Note: In verse 15 the **depths of the earth** is probably a poetic phrase for the womb from the point of view of the embryo.*

10. What change of attitude is evident in verses 17, 18?

Read Psalm 139:19-24

11. What sudden thought comes to the psalmist as he begins to see something of the omniscience, omnipresence, and creative power of God?

Note: Omniscience--the quality of having universal knowledge, infinitely wise. Omnipresence--the quality of being present everywhere at the same time.

What is the essence of the sin of the wicked people he describes?

12. With whom does the psalmist now identify himself?

13. How do you account for the change of mood in the psalmist (verses 23, 24)?

14. On the basis of all the psalmist has realized about God and himself, what petitions does he now make?

Summary

1. How do people you know try to run away from God?

2. How does the realization that God created you, that he is always present, and that he knows everything about you, even your unspoken thoughts, affect you?

Reasons for Praise

Psalm 145

T his great psalm of praise is the first of six which conclude the book of Psalms. Romans 4:20, 21 says that Abraham **grew strong in his faith as he gave glory to God, fully convinced that God was able to do what he had promised** *(RSV)*. Expressions of praise not only please God, but also strengthen our faith. In this psalm, you'll see how praise becomes a major part of prayer and permeates a person's life.

Read Psalm 145:1-7

1. What does it mean to **extol** and **bless**?

    Why is the psalmist moved to praise God?

2. What names for God does the psalmist use?

Note: **LORD**—*the equivalent Hebrew word is Jehovah, meaning "the self-existent (eternal) One who reveals himself." **God**—the equivalent Hebrew word is Elohim, meaning "the strong faithful One."*

3. What verbs does the psalmist use to describe how God's greatness should be published?

By whom should this be done?

Read Psalm 145:8-13

4. What additional reasons for praise are mentioned in this section?

5. What responsibility do the saints of the LORD have?

    How could you help others know something of God's kingdom and power and mighty deeds?

6. How is God praised when we tell others about him?

Read Psalm 145:14-21

7. What new reasons for praise are mentioned?

8. How is the goodness of the LORD revealed to all?

9. What blessings from the LORD are conditional?

    What are the conditions on which these blessings depend?

10. In view of the statements of universal blessings in verses 14-17, what kind of preservation and what kind of destruction must be referred to in verse 20?

11. How do the special conditional blessings exceed the general blessings?

    Why, do you think, are these blessings conditional?

12. What promise and what invitation conclude the psalm?

Summary

1. Why is praising another, even God, difficult?

2. List as many reasons as you can discover in this psalm to praise God:

   -for his being.

   -for his character.

   -for his works.

   Ask each person to read something from his or her list as part of a closing prayer of praise and worship.

   You may want to use your list as an aid to worship in your personal daily prayers this week.

The Hebrew word translated *proverb* means a comparison or simile. It can include a parable, allegory or a short pithy saying. The book of Proverbs is a collection of wisdom sayings in poetic form, the distilled wisdom of teachers who knew the law of God and applied its principles to the whole of life. The purpose of the book of Proverbs is to make the reader wise and strong in character.

The wise men or sages were counselors, perhaps retired civil servants of Israel, who shared their wide experience and judgment as guests in homes or visitors in synagogues, in public squares or on street corners. They sought to make fools wise, to reprove, correct, instruct—to educate for life. They supplemented the ministry of the priests, and interpreted the message of the prophets to the ordinary person. The sages showed that religion involved one's whole life, a total commitment to God. They explained God's relation to human beings and their duty toward God. One central theme permeates the whole book, *The fear of the LORD is the beginning (foundation) of wisdom.*

Section headings in Proverbs ascribe particular parts to different people—Solomon, the wise, Agur, and Lemuel. The general title in Proverbs 1:1 indicates, not that Solomon wrote the whole book, but that he contributed the larger part, and was the most noted figure in proverbial lore.

The questions in this study guide assume the use of a recent translation such as the New International Version, Revised Standard Version, the New English Bible, or the Jerusalem Bible.

Preparation

These studies in Proverbs will be more meaningful if you set aside a time every day to read, meditate, and pray over the sections for the next week's study. In some of the studies (such as Discussion 18) there are a number of references to other related Bible passages. One small section and its cross references will be sufficient for one day's meditation. Proverbs make a rich diet. You will find a short section each day more digestible than attempting a whole study at one sitting.

The Purpose of the Proverbs

Proverbs 1:1-7; 2:1-22

The book of Proverbs is an open door to the wisdom of many generations. Take the opportunity these studies provide to build this knowledge into the foundation of your life.

Read Proverbs 1:1-7

1. Verse 1 is the general title of the book. For background on Solomon read 1 Kings 3:5-14, 28 and 4:29-34.

    What was the source and extent of Solomon's wisdom?

    Why had Solomon requested it?

2. For what four types of people are these proverbs written?

    For what purpose in each specific case?

    How do these purposes differ in their shades of meaning? Use a dictionary to help you understand these words more fully.

3. What is the starting point of all true knowledge?

    What does this expression **the fear of the LORD** mean to you?

    *Note: **fear** is used here in the sense of <u>reverent awe</u>. Verse 7 is the foundation of the whole book of the Proverbs.*

4. What does Proverbs 9:10 add to your understanding of 1:7?

    In view of this, what advice would you give to the leaders of our nation and others trying to solve great international problems?

    Who rejects the wisdom and instruction of God?

Read Proverbs 2:1-22

5. What is required of the person who desires wisdom (verses 1-4)?

6. Why can't human beings attain wisdom without God?

    What actions of the LORD are described in verses 6-8?

    Upon whose behalf does he act?

8. What benefits will follow for your mind, your heart, your soul and your whole being (verses 9-15)?

    From what evil will you be protected?

9. How are evil men described?

   How is the loose (adulterous) woman described?

10. What further benefits do verses 20, 21 add to those described in verses 9-11?

11. What are the results of the two ways of life contrasted in verses 20-22?

Summary

1. From this study what do you learn about the pursuit of wisdom?

   What do you learn about the nature and source of wisdom?

   What do you learn about the rewards of wisdom?

2. How can you use these insights in teaching your children?

3. What, do you think, is the difference between knowledge and wisdom?

Trust and Obedience

Proverbs 3:1-35

Trust in God and obedience to him are the foundations of the Christian life and practice. If you apply the teachings in Proverbs 3 to your life, you will experience God's promised blessings.

Read Proverbs 3:1-10

1. What are the five sets of commands and their accompanying promises?

2. Whom does the first set of commands involve (verse 1)?

    What is obedience's reward?

3. In the second set of commands (verses 3, 4) what relation do you see between the command and the result of obedience to it?

    What do Deuteronomy 7:9 and 32:4 add to your understanding?

4. The next three sets of commands concern attitudes toward self and toward the LORD. What are they?

Which of the promised results have you seen in your life or the life of someone else?

5.   What does the word *all* in verses 5, 6, 9 indicate?

Read Proverbs 3:11-20

6.   What effect does the writer achieve by opening each section of this chapter (verses 1, 11, 21) with the direct address, *My son*?

7.   What is the motive and purpose of the LORD's discipline?

   What does Hebrews 12:5-11 add to the meaning of discipline?

   In both sections, what response to discipline is required?

8.   Verses 13-20 are a parenthetical portion about the virtues of wisdom.   What are the benefits of wisdom?

   To what things is wisdom superior?

Read Proverbs 3:21-35

9.   How are the problems of insecurity, anxiety, insomnia, and nightmares answered in verses 21-24?

10.   What positive commands can you rephrase from the negative commands in verses 25-32?

Compare:

-verses 25, 26 with Psalm 91:5-8.

-verses 27, 28 with Galatians 6:10 and Hebrews 13:16.

-verses 29, 30 with Romans 13:8-10.

-verses 31-34 with Psalm 73:2-20.

11. What explanations or reasons accompany the commands in verses 25-32?

What type of relationship does verse 26a and 32b each describe?

12. How is the experience of the righteous, the humble, and the wise different from that of the wicked, the mockers and the fools?

Summary

1. This passage applies trust in God to many areas of life: guidance, wisdom, food, health, discipline, discernment, security, generosity, integrity. What positive example have you seen of a person trusting God in any of these areas?

2. In what situation in your life should this study make a difference this week?

Righteousness and Wickedness

Proverbs 6:16-19; 11:1-31

T he character and results of righteousness and wickedness form one of the basic themes of Proverbs. The book aims to inculcate those virtues commanded throughout the whole Bible. In a day when many deny the existence of absolute standards, Christians need to look squarely at the standards of righteousness revealed in the Scriptures.

Read Proverbs 6:16-19

1. Into what context does verse 16 set the description of wickedness which follows?

   How does the dictionary define *abomination (RSV)* or *detestable*?

2. What parts of the body are mentioned?

   What evil is expressed through each?

3. What single words or brief phrases can you use to describe each of these evils?

4. Since each of these parts of the body may also be vehicles for the expression of righteousness, what righteous acts could replace the wicked ones described?

    What does the Lord Jesus say about these same issues in Matthew 5:1-10?

Read Proverbs 11:1-8

5. What area of daily life deals with balances and weights?

    What current examples of a false balance and a just weight can you give?

    How could you use this section when talking with the person who says it is impossible to be a Christian in today's business world?

6. What are the consequences of the two ways of life described in verse 2?

    How have you seen this demonstrated in life?

7. What are the personal results to the righteous and to the wicked because of their ways of life (verses 3-8)?

Read Proverbs 11:9-14

8. How are others (a neighbor, a city, a nation) affected by the righteous and by the wicked?

9. What sins of the tongue are described here?

How have you learned to hold your tongue and to keep confidences?

Read Proverbs 11:17-21, 23

10. In each of these verses, what contrasts are made?

    In each case what are the results for the different people involved?

11. What does it mean that a mind or heart is *perverse* (verse 20)?

    What does the New Testament description of such a person add to your understanding (Romans 8:5-8)?

Read Proverbs 11:24-31

12. In verses 24-28 what part do material things have in the expression of righteousness and wickedness?

    What principles can you discover for the use of material wealth?

13. What will be the results for one who creates trouble and discord in his own home?

    How do people cause disharmony in their families today?

14. How do Ecclesiastes 12:14 and 1 Peter 4:17, 18 answer the question of the seeming prosperity of the wicked (verse 31)?

Summary

Read again Proverbs 6:16-19 and 11:1 and 20.

Conclude by reading aloud Frances Havergal's hymn, "Take my life and let it be consecrated, Lord, to thee."

"Take my life, and let it be
Consecrated, Lord, to thee;
Take my moments and my days,
Let them flow in ceaseless praise.

Take my hands, and let them move
At the impulse of Thy love;
Take my feet, and let them be
Swift and beautiful for Thee.

Take my voice, and let me sing
Always, only, for my King;
Take my lips, and let them be
Filled with messages from Thee.

Take my silver and my gold:
Not a mite would I withhold;
Take my intellect, and use
Ev-'ry pow'r as Thou shalt choose.

Take my will, and make it Thine,
It shall be no longer mine;
Take my heart, it is Thine own,
It shall be Thy royal throne.

Take my love, my Lord, I pour
At Thy feet its treasure store;
Take myself, and I will be,
Ever, only, all for Thee."

Choices in Life

Proverbs 16:1-9, 16-20;
21:2-8, 13, 16, 17, 21, 23, 24, 26-31

The decisions a person makes determine his or her way of life. The Bible provides a handbook of principles to guide you in your life choices.

Read Proverbs 16:1-9, 16-20

1. How are a person's free will and the sovereignty of God dealt with in these verses?

2. What types of sins are warned against?

3. What actions lead to choices God can bless (verses 3, 6, 7, 8, 16, 17, 19, 20)?

4. What things are promised to the person who obeys God in life's choices?

5. What example have you seen of God's blessing on the right choices a person has made?

Read Proverbs 21:2-8

6. What do verses 21:2 and 16:2 show about the importance of the motives behind our choices?

What do 21:3 and I Samuel 16:6, 7 add to this line of thought?

7. What ways of getting ahead in life are pursued by those who refuse to choose righteousness and justice?

    What are the results (verses 5-8)?

Read Proverbs 21:13, 16, 17, 21, 23, 24

8. What attitudes or choices are expressed in these six verses?

    What are the results of these choices?

9. How would you characterize each verse as a description of a person who loves something in particular?

    What are some of the things loved by the people whom you know?

    Which of these things do you love?

Read Proverbs 21:26-31

10. What contrasts are drawn in verses 26, 28, 29?

11. What do verses 21:27 and 21:3 indicate about the LORD?

    What does God desire from a person?

    What does 1 Samuel 15:22, 23 add to your understanding?

12. How can even our sacrifice and the performance of religious exercises be an abomination to the LORD?

13. What happens when a person plans her or his life without God or against God (verses 30, 31)?

    What evidence have you seen that *nothing prevails against God and nothing avails without him*?

Summary

1. What choices are described in Joshua 24: 14, 15; and Mark 8:34-38?

2. What do these choices cost?

The Human Tongue

Selected Proverbs

We all make mistakes in all kinds of ways, but the man who can claim that he never says the wrong thing can consider himself perfect, for if he can control his tongue he can control every other part of his personality! ...The human tongue is physically small, but what tremendous effects it can boast of! ... Beasts, birds, reptiles and all kinds of sea-creatures can be, and in fact are, tamed by man, but no one can tame the human tongue (James 3:2, 5-8, Phillips' translation).

Set a guard over my mouth, O LORD; keep watch over the door of my lips! (Psalm 141:3).

Misuses of the Tongue

1. What various misuses of the tongue are mentioned in Proverbs 10:18; 12:19, 22; 16:28; 17:5; 19:9; and 20:19?

   What are the results of using the tongue in these ways?

2. What is the LORD's attitude toward these things?

3. What additional misuses of the tongue are mentioned in these Proverbs 25:14; 26:17-23, 28; 27:1, 2 and 28:23?

4. What types of people are described in 26:17-23?

   What does each word picture add to your understanding of the dangers or evils of these misuses of the tongue?

5. What do verses 26:28; 27:1, 2, and 28:23 teach about boasting, self-praise, and flattery?

   Use a dictionary to define *flattery*.

The Tongue's Great Power for Good or Evil

6. In Proverbs 10:11, 20, 21 what are the three virtues of a tongue rightly used?

   How can words bring life, beauty and nourishment?

7. In Proverbs 12:18 and 15:1, 2, 4 what four negative things may happen from the use of the tongue?

   How would you define each of these kinds of words? Use a dictionary.

   From these same verses, how are healing, peace, knowledge, and life brought about?

8. What do Proverbs 18:4, 20, 21 tell of the significance of words in a person's life?

   What powers do words have over the person speaking?

9. In Proverbs 16:24 and 25:11-13 how are good words and their benefits described?

10. How have the right words brought sweetness, health, beauty, wealth, or refreshing to you?

The Importance of Silence and Listening

11. How would you use Proverbs 10:19 to arbitrate quarrels between children, especially brothers and sisters?

12. What practical reasons are given in Proverbs 12:23; 17:27, 28; 18:13; and 21:23 for keeping silent?

13. What is the significance of our response to others' tongues (Proverbs 17:4)?

    How can you keep from listening to evil, gossip, filth, etc. (Philippians 4:8)?

Summary

1. What are the ways the tongue can get you into trouble?

2. How can you get a tongue that is wise and helpful (Isaiah 50:4, 5)?

3. In closing prayer ask God's help for the wise control and use of your tongue.

Parents, Children, and Youth

Selected Proverbs

The Bible regards children as gifts from the LORD (Psalm 127:3). It holds parents responsible to *bring them up in the discipline and instruction of the LORD* (Ephesians 6:4, RSV). It commands children, in reponse to this care, to obey their *parents as the LORD's representatives* (Ephesians 6:1, Berkeley Version).

Today, fractured marriages, poor communication between generations and lack of respect toward authority characterize our culture. This study offers help and encouragement to parents and children to recognize and fulfill their responsibilities.

Advice for Parents

1. According to Proverbs 13:24; 19:18; 22:6, 15; 23:13, 14; and 29:15, 17, what responsibility do parents have and why?

2. The Bible mentions the rod as a means of discipline. What various kinds of discipline are effective for different children?

3. What do 22:6, 15 and 29:15 teach about children?

4. These verses point out that parents slack in discipline are also slack in love for their children. How have you seen love and discipline expressed together?

Advice for Youth

5. What should a young person do in the face of temptation (Proverbs 1:8-19)? Why?

    What do tempters promise?

6. In Proverbs 4:20-27 what advice is given for each of the parts of the body mentioned?

    What does Jesus teach on this in Matthew 15:11, 15-20?

7. In Proverbs 6:20-24 what benefits result from obedience to parents' teaching?

Note: Deuteronomy 5:1-22; 6:1, 4-9 gives the content of the godly Israelite parents' teaching.

8. In Proverbs 23:15-26 what effects does a child's obedience have upon his parents?

    What attitudes ought children to have toward their parents?

9. What attitudes and company is the young person warned to avoid in Proverbs 23:17-21? Why?

Relationships

10. What attitudes and actions are described in Proverbs 19:26; 20:20; 28:24; and 30:17?

    What accusation or punishment is stated in each case?

11. What do 28:24 and the words of Jesus in Mark 7:9-13 teach about the proper attitude and actions required of a child toward his parents?

12. How does the New Testament express the proper relationship between children and parents (Ephesians 6:1-4; Colossians 3:20, 21)?

Summary

1. From the advice in these passages how can you give spiritual and moral instruction and discipline to children and young people in your family, neighborhood, and community?

2. What, do you think, are the most significant influences on youth today?

    How can parents and the church make a greater impact for God on them?

Womanhood

Selected Proverbs

The status of women historically reflects the moral and spiritual condition of a nation. Some cultures consider women of less value than cattle. Others assign women the position of matriarchs. The Judeo-Christian tradition holds womanhood in honor but the honor carries deep responsibility. Problems arise in the home, the tribe, and the nation when woman's role is corrupted or when woman herself becomes corrupt.

The Immoral Woman

1. How is the immoral (adulterous) woman described in Proverbs 2:16-19; 5:3-6; and 6:23-29, 32, especially her speech and her path?

    What are the effects and results of the adulterer's way of life?

2. Why is her sin against her husband also a sin against God (2:17 and Exodus 20:14)?

3. From these passages, what attitude does the Bible take toward sexual relations outside of marriage?

The Quarrelsome Woman

4. What does the vivid picture in Proverbs 11:22 teach?

   How would you define *discretion*?

5. What is the central thought common to Proverbs 19:13; 21:9, 19; and 27:15, 16?

   What effects does a quarrelsome, contentious woman have on others?

6. Why, do you think, is this particular characteristic mentioned so many times?

   How may a woman learn to stop being irritable, particularly in the home (Psalm 34:1; 141:3; Philippians 4:6-8)?

The Good Woman

7. In contrast to the effects of a quarrelsome woman what is said about a good wife (Proverbs 12:4a; 18:22; and 19:14)?

   What kind of person do you think this sort of woman would be?

8. What is the value of a good wife (Proverbs 31:10-31)?

   What is the effect of her life, described in verses 10-12?

9. What are her areas of responsibility (verses 13-24)?

What indicates the degree of her devotion (verses 15, 17, 18, 27)?

10. What responsibility does she take outside her home (31:20)?

   How does her life reflect upon her husband?

11. What does 31:25-27 reveal about this woman's personality?

   What attitudes toward life would such a woman convey to her family?

12. What are the rewards for the good wife and mother (verses 28-31)?

13. How does 31:30 contradict much advice given to women today?

   How can you help girls or young women in your circle of influence to understand the truth of this verse?

Summary

1. How would you define the special contribution that the Christian woman has to make in the home, the community, the world?

2. From this study what evils should a woman avoid and for what good qualities should she aim?

What Should Our Group Study Next?

New Groups and
Outreach Groups

How To Start A Neighborhood Bible Study
Mark *(recommended as first unit of study)*
Acts
John, Book 1 *(Chapters 1-10)*
John, Book 2 *(Chapters 11-21)*
Four Men of God
(Abraham, Joseph, Moses, David)
Romans
1 John and James
Genesis *(Chapters 1-13)*

Groups Reaching
People from
Non-Christian
Cultures

Genesis *(Chapters 1-13)*
Mark
Four Men of God
(Abraham, Joseph, Moses, David)
Romans

Advanced Groups/
Sunday School
(Adult and Older
Teens)

Matthew Book 1 *(Chapters 1-16)*
Matthew Book 2 *(Chapters 17-28)*
Courage to Cope
Four Men of God
(Abraham, Joseph, Moses, David)
1 & 2 Peter *(Letters to People in Trouble)*
Hebrews
The Coming of the Lord
(1 & 2 Thessalonians, 2 & 3 John, Jude)
Prophets of Hope *(Haggai, Zechariah, Malachi)*
Promises from God
Servants of the Lord
Work - God's Gift

Biweekly or
Monthly Groups

They Met Jesus
(Eight Studies of New Testament Characters)
Celebrate
Courage to Cope
Psalms and Proverbs
Servants of the Lord
Work - God's Gift

ALL studies in this series available from:

Neighborhood Bible Studies
34 Main Street
Dobbs Ferry, New York 10522
800-369-0307

About Neighborhood Bible Studies

Neighborhood Bible Studies, Inc. is a leader in the field of small group Bible studies. Since 1960, NBS has pioneered the development of Bible study groups that encourage each member to participate in the leadership of the discussion.

The **ministry** of Neighborhood Bible Studies is providing people the opportunity to discover the truths of Scripture for themselves. Through these small group discussion Bible studies, people:

- encounter Jesus Christ
- choose to obey him
- mature in faith.

NBS **methods** and **materials** are used around the world to:

- equip individuals for facilitating discovery Bible studies
- serve as a resource to the church.

Skilled NBS personnel conduct workshops and seminars to train individuals, clergy and laity in how to establish small group Bible studies in neighborhoods, churches, work places and specialized facilities. Publication in more than 35 languages indicates the cross-cultural usability.

Churches from a wide range of denominations use the NBS materials and methods to:

- develop a program of outreach Bible studies
- give electives for high school and adult classes
- build support groups within the church fellowship to encourage spiritual nourishment.

About the Authors

Marilyn Kunz and **Catherine Schell**, authors of the NBS series of discussion guides, founded Neighborhood Bible Studies and directed its work for thirty-one years.

COMPLETE LISTING of NBS STUDY GUIDES

Getting Started
How To Start a Neighborhood Bible Study *handbook & cassette*

Bible Book Studies
Genesis, Chapters 1-13   *Beginnings with God*
Psalms and Proverbs *Perspective and Wisdom for Today*
Isaiah   *God's Help is On the Way*
Haggai, Zechariah, and Malachi *Prophets of Hope*
Matthew Book One   *God's Promise Fulfilled*
Matthew Book Two   *God's Purpose Fulfilled*
Mark   *Discovering Jesus Today*
Luke   *Good News and Great Joy*
John Book One   *Believe and See*
John Book Two   *Believe and Live*
Acts Book One   *A New Beginning*
Acts Book Two   *Paul Sets the Pattern*
Romans   *A Reasoned Faith...   ...A Reasonable Faith*
1 Corinthians   *A Challenge to Maturity*
2 Corinthians/Galatians   *A Call for Help and Freedom*
Ephesians/Philemon   *Living out God's Purposes*
Philippians/Colossians   *Letters from Prison*
1 & 2 Thessalonians, 2 & 3 John, Jude   *The Coming of the Lord*
Hebrews   *Unveiling Jesus Christ*
1 & 2 Peter   *Letters to People in Trouble*
1 John and James   *Faith that Knows and Shows*

Topical Studies
Stress   *Bible Leaders Who Coped*
Celebrate   *Reasons for Hurrah's*
Courage to Cope   *Uncommon Resources*
Promises From God   *Hope that Doesn't Disappoint*
Servants of the Lord   *Living by God's Agenda*
Set Free   *Leaving Negative Emotions Behind*
Work - God's Gift   *Life-Changing Choices*

Character Studies
Four Men of God   *Unlikely Leaders*
Lifestyles of Faith Book One   *Choosing to Trust God*
Lifestyles of Faith Book Two   *Choosing to Trust God*
They Met Jesus   *Life-Changing Encounters*